Woven Threads

Woven Threads

Inspirational Stories of Real Life Divine Appointments

Mary Hicks

XULON PRESS

Xulon Press
2301 Lucien Way #415
Maitland, FL 32751
407.339.4217
www.xulonpress.com

Julie Hansen Bush has been a life long artist in multiple mediums. Her digital watercolor, calligraphy and embroidery are shown on the front and back covers. You can find her on Facebook @JulieHansenBushStudios or on Instagram@juliehbush

Unless otherwise indicated, Scripture quotations taken from the Holy Bible, New Living Translation (NLT). Copyright ©1996, 2004, 2007 by Tyndale House Foundation. Used by permission of Tyndale House Publishers, Inc.

Printed in the United States of America.

Paperback ISBN-13: 978-1-63221-170-5
eBook ISBN-13: 978-1-6322-1501-7

TABLE OF CONTENTS

♡

"And we know that God causes everything to work together for the good of those who love God and are called according to His purpose."
Romans 8:28

INTRODUCTION

"My Heart is at Your Service"
– William Shakespeare (goodreads.com)

Have you ever stopped to wonder if a chance encounter had meaning? Perhaps you see someone, a complete stranger, and feel a sudden urge, a nudge, and a tug inside of your heart telling you to speak to him or her? Have you ever been out somewhere and bumped into someone coincidentally, perhaps someone you haven't seen in a long time? Was it a friend you had been thinking about that morning; and later that afternoon you magically run into him or her at the grocery store? If you're like me, we all have had moments when these situations and feelings occur. I like to call them divine appointments and I have learned to be open and available when I get the urge to simply smile or say hello. Actions matter. Words matter.

The powerful words both spoken or written to you from a trusted friend, a parent, a coach, or a teacher or even a stranger can speak life into you. Words and actions have the power to give life to our dreams, our calling and our passion. Be intentional when choosing your words. Those seemingly small and insignificant moments when we are able to share an encouraging word, or lend a helping hand, could lead to something of eternal significance for someone. We are often too busy and self-focused to show compassion to those

God has placed in our paths. We become so caught up in our own needs and plans and we do not see the needs of others. The fast-paced world in which we live in is in desperate need of love and compassion. People need people and were created for a relationship with both our creator and others. I believe we were put on this earth to notice others, to engage with and learn from them and grow us as individuals. The very people we develop a relationship with are a part of God's plan for our lives. Some of the people we meet are there for a short time, others for a lifetime. Random, you might say, happenstance? I think not. None of us can control fate or chance. No one, that is, but God. If you look back over the course of your life, you may question why certain things have happened. Many times things do not turn out like we expect, but we must learn to trust that perhaps God has something better in store for us. He has a specific plan and purpose for everything. Life can be hard, challenging, and disappointing. So often God doesn't change things, but he can change us. You and I have the ability to change how we respond and react to both challenging circumstances and difficult people. My prayer each day is that I ask God to use me to be an encouragement to someone else. It comes as no surprise that when we ask, He will equip us and provide those opportunities. It is up to us to be willing to be used by God and trust that He will guide us. God is the master weaver, continually weaving people in and out of our lives to grow us, to teach us something about ourselves, and our world. He has the power to change the trajectory of our lives.

In the upcoming pages, I urge you to open your mind and heart to all God has for you. I have described how some of the seemingly random encounters and "chance" meetings have impacted my life. I am certain that I have had divine appointments and believe beyond a shadow of a doubt that God has been the author of these appointments. Like our pain and our heartaches, God interlaces those ripped and ragged threads together with the smooth, silky, rich, and colorful threads of joy and love to create the grand design of our lives. We cannot begin to fathom the work of art He is creating in us. He has a specific purpose for our existence on this earth, and we need to be confident in His plan. God has taken me to so many amazing places, strategically putting so many special people along my path, and for that I am so grateful and blessed.

"Your time on this earth is a gift to be used wisely. Don't squander your words or your thoughts. Consider that even the simplest actions you take for your lives matter, beyond measure, and they matter forever" (Andrews, *The Noticer*, 2009).

"The LORD directs the steps of the Godly. He delights in every detail of their lives." Psalm 37:23

WOVEN BEGINNINGS
CANADA

*a*ll of my life, I have been fortunate to be surrounded by a lot of good friends. Growing up in a small Canadian town, my parents made sure I could try my hand at most anything, from piano lessons, choir, swimming, to ice skating, track and field, basketball, and volleyball. It is incredible to think that forty-six years ago Susan and I met on the playground chasing boys! As our friendship grew, we both realized we had a lot in common. We loved sports and competition, even if it was for the boys. When we hit middle school, (which in Canada is grades 6 through 8) we spent our days in class, but after school, you could find us tobogganing or skating on an ice rink together. We were inseparable. Even our weekends consisted of slumber parties and long bike rides. When we reached high school, we tried out for as many sports teams as we could: Susan the tall, long-legged blonde, and I, in comparison, was the short, dark-headed one. The high school system at the time consisted of grades 9 through 13. You could graduate after grade 12 and enter junior college, but in order to be admitted to a four-year university you were required to graduate from grade 13. Susan graduated after grade 12 and I stayed behind for another year of high school, as I was unsure of a career path. Even though miles separated us, we continued to stay in touch and would reunite over the summers. One summer when Susan was home from college, her dad mentioned to me that there was a handsome, American guy doing some work at a large company her dad managed. Since Susan and her sister both had steady boyfriends, her dad knew that I was "available." It was this particulate summer I met him.

"A friend is always loyal, and a brother is born to help in time of need." Proverbs 17:17

WOVEN HEART STRINGS

♡

*T*he year 1983 was a defining year in my life. As a little girl growing up in Canada, I could only dream of one day finding my Prince Charming and running off into the sunset to spend the rest of my life with him. I was twenty-one, home from college for the summer and waiting tables at a local restaurant when a group of three men sat in my section. As I approached the table, I knew one of the gentlemen (Susan's dad), and he began to introduce me to the other two fellows. I was immediately drawn to the one with the kind face, welcoming smile, and charming Southern accent. As I nervously served lunch to this friendly group of men, I could sense that I wanted to find out more about the Southern gentleman, Mitchell. I had to know more about this intriguing, handsome guy. Well, believe it or not, as "plans" would have it, serving lunch to this Southern gentleman soon developed into a relationship. I actually ended up asking him out on a date to a friend's wedding shower. I was smitten and knew in my heart that Mitchell was the one for me. But there was one small problem. His work assignment in Canada was not permanent. He would only be staying for twelve months. Over the course of the following months, we spent a lot of free time together. My family grew to love him and welcomed him with open arms. I was head over heels in love. I knew the day was coming when he would be leaving, heading back to the US for a few short weeks and then packing his bags for a yearlong work assignment in Australia. As he pulled out of my driveway, leaving Canada and me behind on that sunny June day, he promised to call me, but my heart was broken. When he arrived in Indiana, he called and asked me to come and see him before he left the United States. The following weekend, my sister and I headed down the interstate to the small town in Indiana where Mitchell was working for a few weeks before moving to his next assignment in Australia. I wanted to see him one last time and, perhaps, he felt the same way. We had a wonderful time together, but the weekend flew by too quickly. I sobbed as my sister and I drove north up the interstate, thinking this could be the last time I would ever see him. A week later, and six weeks before Mitchell's journey to Australia, I invited him to come back to Canada to Susan's sister's wedding. He not only came, but he surprised me on the Saturday of the wedding. Little did I know but he had been planning all along to propose to me that weekend. Six weeks later Mitchell and I were married in a beautiful ceremony in my parent's backyard and literally ended up truly flying off into the sunset from Canada to Australia. When I think back on how wildly spontaneous our eleven-month courtship was and where it took us, I am in awe. I didn't know how or when I would meet "the one," but God knew who I needed; and I am so blessed Mitchell was sent my way in a most extraordinary manner. How could it be, or was it just "chance" that I met the man of my dreams from a small town in Arkansas while waiting tables in Stratford, Ontario, Canada? I was discovering, but not fully comprehending that my life was not merely an unplanned journey of coincidences.

"For I know the plans I have for you, says the Lord. They are plans for good and not for disaster, to give you a future and a hope."

Jeremiah 29:11

MY HOPES, GOD'S PLANS

♡

I'm not sure if my parents prayed that God would provide me with a spouse who would complete me; if so, I am confident their prayers were answered. Regardless, Jeremiah 29:11 was fulfilled in my life: "For I know the plans I have for you, says the Lord, they are plans for good and not for disaster, to give you a future and a hope." This Scripture carries weighted meaning throughout our lifetimes. Having faith in God is not just for those times to get us through the rough patches and the inevitable challenges of life, but to be with us in every part of our journey along the way. His plan is working in us daily, and He desires each of us to be open to a relationship with Him. It wasn't until I married the exact person God had in mind for me that I began to learn of Jesus and His amazing and saving grace. Mitchell and I come from different backgrounds, as well as different countries. Without a doubt, I wholeheartedly believe that he and I were destined for each other. Mitchell was raised in the Deep South in Southern Arkansas, while I grew up in the South also… but Southern Ontario, Canada! I now proclaim to have a "Southern Canadian accent." Early on in our marriage, Mitchell and I would read the Bible together starting from the book of Genesis. We truly were beginning a new life as a young married couple and moving halfway around the world to begin our journey together. Our year in Australia was exciting and really did seem like a yearlong honeymoon! We lived in a cute little "flat," on the shores of the beautiful beige, sandy beach on the Gulf of St. Vincent in Adelaide, Australia. Our weekends consisted of exploring God's beautiful creation in "the land down under." The Australian people were incredibly welcoming and kind. Looking back, I see the very people God was placing in my life during our first year of marriage. God sent me the gift of a wonderful, older Australian lady, Veronica, who became a mentor and close friend. She and her husband embraced Mitchell and I into their family that year as our surrogate family. To leave home at twenty-two years of age and move halfway around the world may seem daunting and scary, but not for me. True love has a way of doing that, of making you feel safe and secure. Previous to this time, I had a short stint at a college in South Florida for a semester, so perhaps this helped prepare me for my journey to "the land down under" a few years later. It was 1984 when we moved to Australia, and back in those days there were no cell phones Skype, or Face Time. I would eagerly look forward to calling home to Canada every Sunday night when rates were the cheapest, only to have a delay on the other end of the phone when I would speak. How far technology has come. From the day I was married and over the course of my life my father has sent me countless handwritten letters lovingly written from his heart. His thoughtful, yet comical notes, drawings and letters have penetrated the depths of my heart and I will cherish them forever. As with what we say, the words we read have the power to influence our minds and penetrate our souls. As it is written in Psalm 19:14 "May the words of my mouth and the meditation of my heart be pleasing to you oh Lord, my rock and my redeemer." While on assignment in Australia, Mitchell worked all day, Monday through Friday, so I had to keep myself busy. I attended aerobics classes and began to make new friends.

During our short engagement and in the first year of our marriage, I never once wavered on my commitment to Mitchell. Living so far away, at such a young age and with no family, we were totally dependent upon each other for everything. Thankfully, I was born with some-what of an outgoing personality. As the saying goes, it seems I "never meet a stranger." I am thankful God gave me this gift, as it has helped me so much after leaving my family and all that was familiar to me in Canada. I think back to how worried my parents must have been sending their spontaneous, twenty-two-year-old, newly married daughter to the other side of the world. One thing I do know is that in the eleven months we dated, my parents grew to love and trust their new son-in-law to take care of their little girl. God was at work and was growing me to be independent, strong, and self-reliant. I had several things to look forward to during our yearlong assignment in

Australia. During that year, we went back to visit Mitchell's family in Arkansas for Christmas, and in the early spring, my mother and a good friend came to visit us in Australia. In all honesty, when August 1985 rolled around, I was ready to come back, but come back to where? The realization hit me. I would not be going back to my home country of Canada, to my family that I was so very close to.

My knowledge of God and true faith was somewhat limited at this point in my life. My faith at this juncture centered on attending church and "religious" activities more than actually having a personal relationship with Jesus Christ. I had wonderful parents, had grown up attending church regularly, been taught right from wrong, and to respect and obey my parents and elders. But as I have found out, something was missing. I was not fully aware of the intimate and deep rela-tionship I could have with my Creator--the one who was divinely weaving together the people and the places that would become so instrumental in my life and my spiritual growth as a person. Maybe God was beginning to open my heart and pursue me in ways I never knew possible. Not maybe, but absolutely.

"Trust in the LORD with all your heart; do not depend on your own understanding. Seek His will in all you do, and He will show you which path to take."
Proverbs 3:5-6

GOD PROVIDES

We crossed continents once again returning from Adelaide, Australia to settle in Atlanta, where the company Mitchell worked for was based. The only time I had been to the state of Georgia was either flying over as I flew back to Canada from college breaks in Florida or driving through while on vacation. I was going to be a "Southern Canadian."

Once again, the thrill of a new place was exciting to me. One of our first tasks was to find housing, so we quickly started our search for a place to call home. We found the perfect place and were so excited to move into our first home in a fast-growing community located in a suburb of North Atlanta. Mitchell's career at this time involved a lot of traveling, usually leaving Sunday night and returning on Friday night. It was lonely for me at first, so I decided to get a job at a local department store in a nearby mall. Mitchell would be gone all week long, which meant I was by myself all week.

Once more, God handed me a new pattern and began weaving new, special people into my life. I was in a new home, a new country, making new friends, and experiencing new places. Very quickly, our new next-door neighbors had become like second parents to me. Their home was a refuge in a thunderstorm and their table a place to share a meal. As I look back, I am certain God placed this loving and generous couple right next door during the first few years of my marriage to help me transition and to navigate everything that was occurring in my life. Their unconditional love for Mitchell and I was not only comforting to us, but also to my parents fifteen hundred miles away. We were fortunate to also have met another neighbor two doors up who became like family to us as well. Only now can I see how each and every person I had met during the early years of my life had "coincidentally" been there for me.

In November of 1988, we were blessed with our first child, a son, Michael. With no family around and Mitchell traveling a lot, our neighbors had become our extended family who guided and supported us during those early years of parenting. They truly were heaven sent, as they unselfishly stepped into our lives and provided guidance and wisdom as a young, newly married couple and as new parents.

"What is always true is that the decisions that we make today determine the stories we tell about our lives tomorrow. Every day, all day, we make one small choice after another. And these choices just keep accumulating, each one woven into the rest, forming the tapestry that is our life story" (Groeschel, Divine Direction, 2016)

A TIME FOR EVERYTHING

Not only did God send us to a neighborhood with some loving and caring next-door neighbors who grew to be like family, I got to know another neighbor from across the street that also became a very special friend. Laurie was that special friend. From the moment I met her, I knew her fun-loving, bubbly personality was one I wanted to connect with right away. Some of my greatest memories are of the two of us walking late into the evening, talking and laughing, catching up on our day. Over the course of the two short years they lived in the neighborhood, Laurie and I became wonderful friends. It was August of 1990, and one memory, to this day, still haunts me. It was the middle of the afternoon and my doorbell rang. I opened the door to see Laurie's husband standing there, his face ashen and his voice trembling. Choking back tears, he went on to tell me a serial killer in Gainesville, Florida had tragically murdered Laurie's only sister. Finally, after weeks of searching, the police received a tip and the monster that ultimately confessed to the murders was finally behind bars. As the news and details of the crime began to surface, my heart broke for my dear friend and her family. I tried to console her as best as I was equipped to do at this time in my life. Not long after this tragic time, Laurie and her husband were transferred out of state with his job. In the months and years that followed, Laurie spent endless days sitting in a crowded courtroom, listening to the gut-wrenching testimony of the very man that took the life of her beautiful sister and four other innocent college students. He pled guilty to the five murders and was convicted and sentenced to death. Over the years and due to the sheer distance and the in the busyness of raising our young families, Laurie and I would connect once or twice a year. I have precious memories of my dear friend Laurie, remembering both the happy and tragic times.

"If you're alone, I'll be your shadow. If you want to cry, I'll be your shoulder. If you want a hug, I'll be your pillow. If you need to be happy, I'll be your smile. But anytime you need a friend, I'll just be me" (Unknown, dailyinspirationquotes.com).

KINDRED SPIRITS

One Friday afternoon after coming in the door from work, Mitchell announced the company he worked for since graduating college had just been bought out and he was without a job. Several weeks earlier, we had planned and paid for our first Caribbean cruise, which was leaving the very next day. Since we had already planned the cruise, we decided we would go anyway. It was on this trip that we met a wonderful couple from Missouri. Ironically, this couple had met our neighbors in the airport a few days prior to our cruise. After much small talk, our neighbor, who claims to know everybody in the world, befriended this couple and found out they were also going on a cruise. Incredibly enough, without any photographs and just a verbal description of my husband and I, this couple found us amongst the 1,500 people on the same ship. The four of us, who were close in age connected immediately, as though we were long-lost friends who had just been reunited! Rhonda's zeal for life and outgoing, fun-loving personality drew me to her immediately. We spent most of the entire week of our vacation together, dancing the "Macarena," sipping iced tea, and singing the latest hit song, "HOT-HOT-HOT!" We enjoyed each other's company so much so, that several months later we planned another vacation together. Not only did Rhonda and I have so much in common, our husbands were kindred spirits. The guys discovered they had both lived in the same freshman dorm at the University of Arkansas many years ago. Mitchell and Terry had such laidback, unassuming demeanors that complimented their zany and outgoing wives. We sensed there was something different about our new friends, ...they had an unshakable faith in God. It resonated from within them in what they said and how they lived out their daily lives. Little did I know but God was continuing to open up my heart, pursuing me as my spiritual journey was taking another step forward. In retrospect, I can see how God was once again weaving and placing just the right people in my path.

Over the course of the next several years we saw each other as much as distance would allow since living several states away. We began taking yearly vacations together and intentionally made time to see each other. Rhonda would send me cards of encouragement as well as Christian music

CDs. As I began to listen to the words of the songs, God's presence continued to stir in my heart. We began to marvel at how "fate" had brought us together all those years ago. One August morning, I received a phone call. The voice on the other end of the phone introduced herself as Rhonda's sister. With her voice breaking up, she told me that Rhonda's husband of 23 years, Terry, had been in a terrible car accident and didn't survive. This set our relationship on a different course. Over the next several weeks and months, we would talk deep into the night as I tried to console my grief-stricken friend. The dynamic of our relationship had changed, as God was beginning to use me to be her confidant and sounding board. The tables had turned. Where God had used her so many times in my life, now, I had the opportunity to be there for her. That chance meeting years before was the beginning of a continual thread, weaving in and out at various points of my life.

"Sometimes you never know the value of a moment until it becomes a memory" *(Dr. Seuss, goodreads.com).*

"So encourage each other and
build each other up, just as
you are already doing."
1 Thessalonians 5:11

MAPPING OUT
OUR JOURNEY

♡

*A*fter returning from the cruise, and as "luck" would have it, Mitchell received a call from a past business associate. This gentleman, who Mitchell had worked for on engineering projects in the past, had a new proposition for Mitchell. This opportunity was to re-engineer a small travel management company he also owned. He was confident Mitchell could help get it "in the black." The good news was Mitchell would have a job;

the bad news was the job was several hours away from our home. Since graduating college, Mitchell had always worked as an engineering consultant so this would be a career change, but he was up for the challenge. His dream had always been to own his own business someday, and this might be the opportunity he had been dreaming of. Since he was a little boy, Mitchell always had a passion for travel, so being involved in helping turn around a travel company was an exciting proposition. Mitchell and I decided this new career path was exactly God's plan for us at this time in our lives. God was beginning to make his dream a reality, and our lives were beginning to change. God was mapping out our journey: a journey full of ups and downs, challenges, as well as new life experiences and opportunities

"We can make our plans, but the
LORD determines our steps."
Proverbs 16:9

TIME FLIES

Over the past thirty-five years, the gentleman who helped make this opportunity possible has become a wonderful mentor and valued friend. There is no doubt that God knew just exactly who to place in Mitchell's path in order to fulfill his dream of owning his own business. Looking back, God has been so faithful in providing us with exceptional employees and clients. It is much different running your own business than working for a large consulting firm, but Mitchell found this a challenge that he embraced enthusiastically and passionately. Early on, he found it took people with a certain level of "servitude" while consistently maintaining a positive mental attitude that would help our business thrive. As is the case with any new company, there are new challenges almost daily. Ours was no exception. It was imperative to remain focused, yet flexible. There was always a need to adjust the business model, adapting and adopting new ways of providing value to our great customers. The old saying "The only thing that is constant is change itself"' is so true with both business and life, but especially in the travel industry.

During the first year of Mitchell's involvement in the travel industry, he began working on securing a business relationship with, what was then, a mid-sized, fast food company based in Atlanta. After more than 36 months, Mitchell finally secured a mutually beneficial alliance. Within a few years, the founder became a valued partner with Mitchell in our travel management company. He wasn't merely a partner in business but perhaps, more importantly; he became a mentor and friend who had an immense influence on both our family's business and in our personal lives. He continued as a valued partner, and true friend, until he passed away in 2014 at the age of 93. Our family will forever be grateful for his impact on our business, our corporate culture, and on our family. God has truly blessed our business and, without question, has seen us through many rewarding and challenging times that has made our family, our employees, and our business stronger.

It was inevitable that the long 70-mile commute meant we would have to move to the town the travel company was located. We put our home on the market, but it took an agonizing two years to sell. I was not happy about having to leave our wonderful neighbors who had become like a second family to us, but we knew it was what we had to do. Not long after moving into a two-story home in the back of a quiet cut-de-sac, I had heard there was a little boy who lived down the street. Being new to this city, I knew it would be imperative for me to make new friends. Without hesitation, I ventured down the street, knocked on their door and introduced myself. Incredibly, this family told me they were going to be building a new home on the lot right beside us in the cul-de-sac. This was the beginning of an amazing life-long friendship that is still going strong to this day. Once again, God provided just who we needed in our lives to help navigate those challenging, yet rewarding, years of parenting. Our children grew up together: building tree houses in the backyard; learning how to ride bikes; playing road hockey and soccer in the cul-de-sac. Reflecting back, we have had many, many years of a wonderful and rich friendship with this remarkable family.

About a year after moving into our new home in south Atlanta, we were blessed with another baby boy, Steven. Even though our two boys are brothers they couldn't be more different; but they are different in so many wonderful ways. The one thing they do have in common is that they grew to know their Savior and Creator. Nothing brings a parent greater joy than to know his/her children have faith in the one who created them.

"Children are a gift from the LORD,
they are a reward from Him."
Psalm 127:3

As a young family having moved into a new area, we knew it was important for us as a family to find a church home. We began attending church and created the opportunity for the boys to get involved in Sunday school and other activities. After attending there for a few years, the associate pastor announced he would be head pastor of a small church that was being planted by our church. We loved our pastor and his quick wit, and incredible heart for God's people. He also had a gift of delivering and sharing a message that related so well to life. Over the course of ten years, this pastor was instrumental in helping me grow my faith and teaching me how to have a personal relationship with my Creator and living every day of my life for Him.

Mitchell and I both decided that this would be a great move for our young and growing family, to help in starting this church plant with our pastor and friend. What started out as a congregation of about fifteen people has grown today to over five hundred in attendance every Sunday. Although the original pastor is no longer there, our current pastor is a wonderful man with a heart for sharing God's love and ministering to His people. As our church grew, so did my faith. I attended weekly Bible studies, continuing to learn more and grow in my faith. My belief is that God created us to know and seek after Him and His will for our lives. He yearned for a relationship with me, and I was learning there was more to life than just going through the motions. My perspective was changing, and my heart was open to that change. On a beautiful, southern, warm summer day after church, I was baptized in our church's swimming pool. Incredibly, our church had been a former NHL hockey practice facility and a former health club, complete with an Olympic-sized swimming pool. And what was so special, and will be for eternity, was that my son Michael and I were baptized together.

The years we spent raising our children seemed to rush by. My mother always told me how quickly children grow up. It wasn't until I experienced this for myself that I realized how right she was. The old saying that the days may seem long, but the years fly by during child-rearing years is so true! As my children continued to grow up, I began to see how God was working not only in my life, but in their lives as well. Our youngest son attended a private Christian school, and it was his second-grade teacher who was instrumental in his faith journey. She was a special lady with an undeniable love for children and a heart for God. My dad had been diagnosed with cancer that year, and this teacher and the class prayed fervently that entire year for my dad's healing. God's answer to all of those prayers miraculously healed him and taught my sweet, little son and our family the power of prayer. It was that year Steven felt that nudge and asked Jesus to come into his heart. Looking back, I not only see the way God was weaving people into my life, but into the lives of my husband as well as our children.

As parents, we are called to give our children strong spiritual foundation. Over the course of our children's lives they will come into contact with many people who will have a profound influence and impact on them. My children are so fortunate to have had many wonderful, caring, and godly teachers, coaches, friends, and mentors who were strategically placed in their lives, guiding, challenging, and growing them to reach their potentials in a positive way.

"Direct your children onto the right path, and when they are older, they will not leave it." Proverbs 22:6

A SIMPLE YES

*I*t had been an extremely stressful week beginning the night my parents flew in from Canada. The night they arrived, my mother's purse containing $1,500.00 was stolen at the airport; the purse was found the next day. The good news, if any, was the thief left her passport and was only interested in the cash. Every day of their "vacation," it seemed something happened that was unpleasant. To heighten the distress of the week, on the last night of their visit, my tiny, but mighty mom had fallen out of bed. My mother always claims she is fine, and this night was no different. It wasn't until the next week after she returned home to Canada that she found out her pelvis was actually cracked. As I drove my parents back to the airport, I was emotionally drained and full of mixed feelings. As I stood watching them walk through the airport security checkpoint, I was sad. I was sad that the past week had been so chaotic and draining when all I wanted was for every precious day spent with my parents to be joyous and happy. It is a strange feeling when you are standing amongst the hubbub in an airport and you have the perception you are a solitary soul standing in the midst of all the commotion. This is how I felt as I watched my parents walking away to board their flight back to Canada. This is when she appeared. I felt a tap on my shoulder and a voice that asked, "Are those your parents?" As I turned, I see this absolutely lovely, African American woman coming toward me with a warm, wide smile. She had a spunky bounce to her step and tight, ringlet curls in her hair. I immediately could feel her warm, vivacious spirit surround me. She worked as a customer service representative at Atlanta Hartsfield-Jackson Airport. She told me she had noticed me as I watched my parents walk away through the airport security. Without much conversation, she boldly asked me if she could pray for my family and me. Yes, right there in the middle of the congested Atlanta airport, perennially ranked the busiest airport in the world! You could ask, what gave her the courage to boldly ask to pray for me, in this environment and at this very moment in time? What was it that drew her to me, when there were thousands of people scurrying around through this gigantic airport? All I could utter was, "Yes." Overcome with emotion, I wept as she began to pray over me. She prayed specifically for things my family and I had been struggling with. During this particular season our family had been going through some very challenging times. How did this woman, a complete stranger, know the details of my family's personal struggles? GOD, that's how. After expressing my gratitude to this kind, obviously incredibly perceptive woman, I stood in the middle of the airport in awe. Our encounter only lasted a few minutes, but little did I know that such a brief, spontaneous encounter and my "yes" to a simple yet, profound prayer could be the beginning of another thread being woven into the tapestry of my life?

"A committed heart does not wait for conditions to be exactly right. Why? Because conditions are never exactly right. Indecision limits The Almighty and His ability to perform miracles in your life. He has put a vision in you... Proceed. To wait, to wonder, to doubt, to be

indecisive is to disobey God" (Andrews, The Traveler's Gift, 2002)

"For GOD is working in you,
giving you the desire and the
power to do what pleases him."
Philippians 2:13

A CHANGE IN PERSPECTIVE

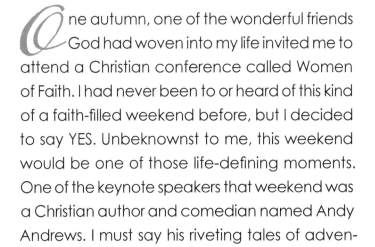

One autumn, one of the wonderful friends God had woven into my life invited me to attend a Christian conference called Women of Faith. I had never been to or heard of this kind of a faith-filled weekend before, but I decided to say YES. Unbeknownst to me, this weekend would be one of those life-defining moments. One of the keynote speakers that weekend was a Christian author and comedian named Andy Andrews. I must say his riveting tales of adventure, intrigue, humor, and wisdom captivated my attention the entire time he spoke. Andy is a well-known author who shares stories about his search for meaning and fulfillment in this outrageous expedition of our existence. After hearing him speak, I was drawn to his words and began to see things around me from a differently. At the end of the conference, I picked up a copy of his book, <u>The Noticer</u>. I read it in its entirety the very next day, which prompted me to subsequently read each of his books. Saying YES to things that come our way can be paramount; for example, my decision to "go to a conference" was one of those defining moments in my life. From that experience forward, I began to see life, and to "notice" the people around me through a different lens and with a new perspective.

"I pray that your hearts will be flooded with light so that you can understand the confident hope He has given to those He called– His holy people who are His rich and glorious inheritance."
Ephesians 1:18

Interestingly, that same year, I had read a book titled Life Without Limits, an autobiography by Nick Vujicic. Nick is an Australian-American Christian evangelist and motivational speaker born with rare disorder, tetra-amelia syndrome. Both The Noticer and Life Without Limits had parallel themes; PURPOSE, particularly finding purpose in your circumstances (2012). I was becoming keenly aware of God quietly nudging me. I began to learn to quiet myself and to take notice of others. A new design was taking shape in me and I started to notice opportunities to reach out and connect with others in spontaneous and unplanned circumstances. As I reflected on past events and relationships, I began to see the pattern God was weaving; those special people and divine circumstances that only God could orchestrate.

"You can make many plans, but the LORDS purpose will prevail."
Proverbs 19:21

A RANDOM MEETING

L ooking back, these were the years of many exciting changes for our family. In the blink of an eye, the boys had grown up. Steven was graduating from high school and Michael was graduating from college. Mitchell was delighted when both boys chose to further their education at the University of Arkansas, his alma mater. Steven was doing his undergraduate studies, while Michael his postgraduate. Now if you knew my husband, you would know he is not just a football fan, he's a "Razorback fanatic."

To say he was thrilled about their choices to attend college at the U of A is an understatement! During our early days dating in Canada, in the middle of a blinding snowstorm, he rode a snowmobile to the nearest hotel that was broadcasting a Hogs bowl game on a TV in their lobby. With the boys both attending the U of A, it seemed natural that Mitchell was not going to pass up the opportunity to purchase season tickets for the football games. In the fall, weekends meant travel: air travel, hotel stays, spending a lot of time in airports. Being that our business is travel management, we fly in and out of the Atlanta airport frequently. Fall rolled around so football season was upon us, which meant another trip to the airport. One particular trip, I decided to pack my copy of The Noticer and my husband packed a book called The Traveler's Gift, both authored by Andy Andrews.

We proceeded toward the entrance to TSA security. I glanced up and saw that sweet, familiar face, with the wide smile and her signature bouncy curls. As I approached the front of the line, there she was. Val, smiling in my direction, made me feel certain she had recognized me. I immediately realized why I was led to pack the book. It wasn't for me this time; it was for Val. I quickly rummaged through my bag to have it ready by the time I reached her. We greeted each other with outstretched arms, and I handed her the book. We quickly exchanged phone numbers, as I had a sense that this was not a "random" meeting. Throughout the course of the next few months, Val would send me encouraging words via text messages. It seemed as though I would receive her words of encouragement at what always seemed to be precisely the perfect day and time.

"Yet God has made everything beautiful for its own time. He has planted eternity in the human heart, but even so, people cannot see the whole scope of God's work, from beginning to end." Ecclesiastes 3:11

A FLUKE?

*W*e all know how important it is to take that last bathroom break before boarding a plane. This time, I was the one waiting on Mitchell outside the men's restroom. As I watched other people passing by, a tall, sandy blonde-haired man bumped into me. He politely excused himself. I glanced up to give the standard, "No problem" reply, when I realized I recognized his face. It was Andy Andrews, the author of *The Noticer*. I quickly introduced myself to him, expressing just how much I enjoyed his books and how his penned words had changed my perspective. I told him I often travel with an extra copy of his book, and that my husband was presently reading one as well. I was completely caught off guard that I forgot to ask him to sign one of the books. With my mind racing, I thought back upon the sequence of events beginning at the Women of Faith conference. What are the chances I would literally bump into the very author whose words on a page had such an impact on how I was seeing people around me so differently than ever before?

Do you believe this was a fluke? Without question, it was not a mere coincidence. The awakening in me that God started at the Women of Faith conference was being reaffirmed in this divine appointment...outside the men's restroom. His divine works were being shown to me so very clearly. I had no doubt that God was up to something!

"When you know that everything matters, that every move counts as much as any other, you will begin living a life of permanent purpose" (*Andrews, The Butterfly Effect, 2010*)

"The LORD will work out his plans for my life - for your faithful love, O LORD, endures forever—dont abandon me, for you made me."

Psalm 138:8

FINDING PATIENCE

♡

ou would think, with the kids in college or on to whatever career path they take, that our "empty nest" life would begin to ease up and slow down. Little did I know my life was not about to ease up from a spiritual perspective? We were still involved in attending basketball games, football games, and everything sending your children to college brings. Little did I know God was preparing me and getting ready to orchestrate a life-changing divine appointment, something that was beyond my wildest imagination.

It was there at a basketball game at the University of Arkansas that I first saw her…her name was Patience. She ran onto the gym floor clapping her hands to cheer and rev up the crowd. With her bright blue eyes, blonde hair, and contagious smile I could sense she was one special girl. I was not just in awe of this young lady because of her talented cheerleading. Patience was an amputee. On her left leg was a zebra-striped prosthetic. She was amazing, and there was something in her spirit that tugged at my heart. As the game went on, her partner would run over and hoist her onto his shoulders. She was thrown high into the air again and again. It was unimaginable to think that she was capable of cheering, especially at the college level. I just sensed there was something special about her, as her spirit soared and reached the audience. As I watched from the stands, I could feel her spirit drawing me in. I wanted to know this proud young lady flipping angelically through the air.

Perhaps God knew my heart's desire, but it would be months before football season and our weekly routine of visiting the boys out in Fayetteville. We routinely stayed at the same hotel when visiting the University of Arkansas, because it was within walking distance to both where the boys lived as well as the football stadium. Arriving for the first game of season, the next morning I headed down to the hotel coffee shop for a quick bite and cup of coffee. I rounded the corner and who do I bump into as she was walking out of the coffee shop? It was the beautiful girl with the striking, bright blue eyes and blonde hair. I could hardly believe my eyes; it was the cheerleader with the zebra-striped prosthetic! My mind raced back to the first moment I saw her cheering from the stands. I stood in awe, knowing I had actually verbalized I wanted to meet her. Not knowing how she would respond, I took a leap of faith and boldly introduced myself. With her beautiful blue eyes dancing, I told her what an inspiration she was to me and all who watched her perform. She simply and kindly responded, "Thank you so much ma'am. You are so kind to say that." It was just a short first meeting, but it was the beginning of another thread being woven into my life. I began piecing the threads together. What could God be up to?

"Therefore I, a prisoner for serving the LORD, beg you to live a life worthy of your calling, for you have been called by GOD."
Ephesians 4:1

Yes, her name is Patience. Let me share with you a little about this beautiful, young woman in her words. She tells it like this:

There it goes again. Another article had come out. This headline hit harder than ever, THE GIRL WITH THE ZEBRA LEG. As a freshman, new to college, and new to this world of independence, I sat with a heavy heart in my dorm room. My name is Patience Beard, and I am the girl with the zebra leg. On April 19, 1994, I was born into this world. On that day, my parents learned that I had something called Proximal Focal Femoral Deficiency, which is just a long term for a short leg. I had PFFD of the left leg. The result of this diagnosis was the amputation of my lower left leg. At eight months old, my first procedure was underway. From this moment on, my life was forever changed, which meant learning and growing to walk and function as normal as possible with a prosthetic leg. Growing up with prosthesis was a challenge. At times, I would question why I was made this way. I would wonder what the point of all of this was. For the most part, I just kept on going as normal as possible. My parents would always say, "God made you special. He made you different for a reason." Those words to me, well, they were just empty. Those words were just as empty as the very life I was living. Upon graduating from high school, I decided to try to carry my love for cheerleading on to college. I made a decision to try out for the University of Arkansas cheerleading team. Through a vigorous tryout process, I made the team. I had finally felt like I had made it, and that my life was about to be complete. I had everything I could have ever wanted--the dream of college, the dream spot as a Razorback cheerleader, and the perfect dorm. I thought I was set. Of course, I was so unaware of the plans that God had for me.

Arriving as a freshman, my first couple months as new college student and as a Razorback cheerleader, I gained a lot of attention for being an amputee. People noticed me more than ever before, and it soon began to bother me more than ever before. I had never felt this way. All of the things that I had thought were going to fill my life with so much joy were doing exactly the opposite. I felt so empty. I began searching deeper for the joy in all the ways of this world. However, thankfully, the Lord had a greater plan for me. I decided to attend a local church in Fayetteville for the first time. As I sat one Wednesday night at our college service, the Lord began to open my eyes to Him. He began stirring my heart to serve Him. As I sat there, I suddenly realized the weight of my sins against such a holy God. I was broken, yet rejoicing in the truth that my life is fully surrendered to a God that loves me, and my life will be forever changed. My hope was now in the

Lord, and that my sins were forever forgiven by the saving grace of Jesus Christ. After that moment, I realized that I was NOT just, "THE GIRL WITH THE ZEBRA LEG." I am now a child of a King, and that my life is for His glory. I could no longer be defined by anything other than a follower of Christ. That, YES, I am that girl with the zebra leg…that, YES, it is a part of me; yet my whole identity is buried deep within Christ Jesus, my Lord and Savior. For the first time in my life the words my parents spoke to me as a child, "God made you this way for a reason," finally made sense to me. I have been incredibly blessed. I did not just lose a leg. I gained a story. A story that can only be told by giving God ALL of the glory…and THAT is exactly why God made me the way He did. I am learning every single day what it means to walk in confidence in Christ and knowing that my identity is in Christ alone. And finally, the one thing that can be seen through human eyes, as a curse is simply a blessing for all and to God be the glory. So, no, I am not just *THE GIRL WITH THE ZEBRA LEG.* I am forgiven, righteous, redeemed, made whole, and a child of the King...all in Christ Jesus!"

"For we are GODS masterpiece. He has created us anew created in Christ Jesus, so we can do the good things He has planned for us long ago." Ephesians 2:10

COINCIDENCE?
RANDOM? CHANCE?

♡

I truly believe that in all those moments in time, God had been behind the scenes orchestrating something divine. These happenings were not just coincidental---my family, my friends; at a restaurant all those years ago, waiting tables and meeting my life partner, Mitchell. Moving to Australia, then to Georgia, our boys choosing to move to a university that was their father's alma mater; Val, Patience, Andy Andrews, each a thread being woven into my life. I felt great clarity in my spirit to be more and more willing to act on and respond to the prompting of the Holy Spirit. For example, I moved immediately on the urgent nudging to dig for that book in my bag when I handed it off to Val. It may have seemed like a small, spontaneous act, but God knew it would eventually fulfill part of a divine plan. It was a precursor for future appointments. I had no idea how God could be orchestrating and aligning everything, even in the lives of three complete strangers.

Over the course of the following months, we were flying fairly frequently, travelling through the airport and it seemed she randomly appear. On one occasion Mitchell, Steven, and I were traveling together. As we rounded the corner, we literally bumped right into my "airport friend" with her welcoming smile. It was as though she knew I was coming. Fast-forward a few months later, several trips in and out of the airport, and no sign of Val. Her encouraging texts had quit. One weekend, I felt that inclination once again stir in my heart. I could not seem to shake the feeling I should try to reach out to her. Up until this point, Val and I had only communicated via text messages. With Val heavy on my heart, I sat in my hotel room and dialed her number; her familiar voice answering on the other end. We had never talked via phone, so I reminded her who I was since it had been six months from our very first encounter. When I asked her if she remembered me, there was no hesitation. She said "Of course!" I asked the usual question of "How are you?" and there was a long pause before she spoke. She replied, "I'm okay now, but I have been in a terrible car accident." There was another long pause as her next words pierced my heart. As if hearing the words in slow motion, she continued on, "I had to have my leg amputated." As my

stomach continued to churn with utter disbe-
lief, I could barely find the words to speak. I
finally responded that I was so sorry to hear
this news. She kindly said, "Don't be sorry for
me. I will be okay. God's got me!" Our bond
was forever sealed, and I knew this was one
very special lady. In the back of my mind, all
I could think about was the first time I met Val,
the books I just "happened" to have read, my
"chance" encounter with Andy Andrews, and
meeting Patience. I had absolutely no doubt
that God had been orchestrating something
much bigger than myself over the last year.
Val was right; God did have her. He had her
from the beginning, and it dawned on me
how blessings can come from painful times
in our lives. I promised Val that I would be in
touch as soon as I returned home from my trip.
Upon returning home, I called Val and, over
the course of the next several months, I made
weekly trips to visit her. She lived about forty

minutes away from me, but I knew God was guiding my every step. Not surprisingly, a few short weeks after her accident her coworkers at the Atlanta airport put on a fundraiser to help cover some of her medical expenses. She called and asked me if I was available to pick her up and attend the fundraiser with her. I happily agreed to assist her in every way I could. I was honored to be part of that special day. I will never forget the number of people that showed up for this event. The outpouring of support for Val was phenomenal. I watched as a steady stream of her airport family came by with well wishes and support. It was not only the people she closely worked with, but also airport management, acquaintances from airlines, and friends she had made throughout her years at the world's busiest airport. It was obvious just how much she was loved and admired and the many lives she had touched.

One Monday, I called to check up on Val to see if I could take her anything. When she answered the phone that day, she told me she didn't want me to come to see her. She said she was "in a bad place," and that her wound was not healing well. Before hanging up the phone, I told her I would be in prayer for her. When I hung up the phone, I was so burdened for her. My heart ached, as I could feel how difficult it was for her to face living life as an amputee. No matter how hard I prayed I still felt there must be something else I could do.

"Do not gloat over me, my enemies! For though I fall, I will rise again. Though I sit in darkness, The LORD will be my light." Micah 7:8

My mind raced back to the divine appointment I had just a few months earlier with Patience. I could begin to see threads were beginning to be woven together. With my youngest son at the University of Arkansas, where Patience also attended, I felt that instant nudge to reach out to him to see if he knew how I could connect with her. I knew they had mutual friends, and perhaps there was someone that knew Patience. Not ten minutes later, I got a text with from my son with Patience's contact information. Without hesitation, I dialed her phone number. I introduced myself and expressed that we had met one time briefly at a hotel coffee shop in Fayetteville. I explained that my son had provided me with her phone number at my request. I shared with Patience about my new friend who had just lost her leg, and I boldly asked her if she could reach out to Val. I had no idea how a young girl would react to such a crazy notion, but her response astounded me. Patience replied, "Mrs. Hicks, I would be happy to call your friend. This is what I live for!"

Over the course of the next several weeks and months, and as Val began to heal, Patience continued to phone Val and encourage her through this process. The day was soon approaching when Val would be fitted for her prosthetic. It would be the start of her new life; the life she accepted, and God had ordained for her. As she calls it, it was her "new normal." You see, Val believes in God and His purpose for her life. She believes His promise that she will never be alone. She knows God will use her and the accident to be a blessing to others.

"But those who trust in the LORD will find new strength. They will soar on wings like eagles. They will run and not grow weary. They will walk and not faint." Isaiah 40:31

It is amazing how one simple "yes" from Patience could be used by God to lead Val out of a place of hopelessness to one of extraordinary healing. Val is one very strong, determined, and independent woman. She relies on God to provide. Not surprisingly, she was back to work at the airport within the year. I continued to check in on both Val and Patience. In the spring of the following year after Val's accident, I thought it would be special for Val and Patience to meet in person. It was on Valentine's Day that Patience flew to Atlanta to meet "her angel" in person. I will never forget the look on Val's face when she saw Patience for the first time. These two incredibly strong and independent women from different backgrounds and different locations across the country now share a bond, a bond that had woven their lives together forever. Just a few months later after Val had received her prosthetic, we were given the opportunity to share our story to a local devotional group. The night before, Val had come to spend the night with us. I got up early that morning and tapped on her door to see if she was ready. As she beckoned me to come in, I saw her standing at the bedside, dressed and ready to go. There was one glaring problem: She could not get her prosthetic on. If the roles had been reversed and this was me, I'm sure I would have either been in tears, or very angry and frustrated, but not Val. You should have seen us. We pushed and we pulled, twisted, and turned. She even tried lying on the bed and I pushed some more. It was quite a scene. After many attempts and afraid of being late to the meeting, Val just looked at me, smiled ever so brightly, and said, "This is not going to stop us from going!" She said, "Grab Mrs. Hopper her crutches. I packed them just in case. I'm ready. Let's go!" I handed her the crutches and off we went. She truly was ready. She was ready to conquer anything that was standing (or in this case...not standing) in her way.

"Dear brothers and sisters, when troubles of any kind come your way, consider it an opportunity for great joy. For you know that when your faith is tested, your endurance has a chance to grow." James 1:2-3

We stood together, Val on her crutches and me by her side, in front of the group and told of our divine appointment the year prior to her horrific accident. The crowd gave her a standing ovation as we stood together, our eyes full of tears. They were tears of joy, of overwhelming gratitude that God had provided for her and restored her life. People came up to speak to Val afterward, giving her words of encouragement and affirmation. I distinctly remember one gentleman who came up and introduced himself to us as a local pastor. He too spoke words of kindness and encouragement to Val. As he walked away, I noticed he had a slight limp. This day truly was the beginning of Val's entrance back into the real world. It would be her new normal, and she embraced it whole-heartedly with such dignity and grace.

"Each time He said, "My grace is all you need. My power works best in weakness." So now I am glad to boast about my weaknesses, so that the power of Christ can work through me."
2 Corinthians 12:9

The following day, I was shopping at our local grocery store and walked up to the deli counter. I glanced down and the man in front of me just so happened to be an amputee! As I approached the counter, I turned to the man and smiled. My jaw dropped as I recognized him. He was the pastor from the devotional group the day before! He smiled back at me and immediately I knew he recognized me as well. He told me how inspired he was listening to Val and our story. I asked him one question:

"You didn't tell us you were an amputee." It just so happened he had long pants on the day of the devotional but this particular day he was in his gym shorts. After a brief conversation, we learned we lived in the very same neighborhood. Over the course of the next several months, on my weekly grocery run, it seemed I would run into my pastor friend. I mentioned that Patience was coming to visit. I could sense he was anxious to meet her, so we made plans for the two of them to meet. He shared his riveting story of how he came to be an amputee and how God had used him since then. He had lost his leg as a young boy to a terrible infection. Incredibly, he went on to be a Paralympics gold medalist. I was in awe of how God was orchestrating and weaving the lives of these remarkable people together, to share their stories of hope and redemption with one another. Coincidence? At this point, I am truly convinced there is no such thing.

That spring, Patience would be graduating from college. She called me one day and said she had applied for an internship in a large church, in of all places, Atlanta. Unbelievably, out of thousands of applicants, Patience was chosen for one of only ten available positions. She would be moving within forty miles of where we lived.

Throughout the next year, Patience became like a daughter to me. It was a natural fit. She would come and bring friends down to our home for weekends, and I would run up to the city to meet her for a quick lunch. Her zeal for life and unshakeable faith in God and His purpose for her life were so inspiring. She would sit on our back deck with her Bible open, praying and journaling. She would always ask me how she could pray for our family and me. Patience's kindness and thoughtfulness was so apparent.

One night, a friend invited me to go with her to the inner-city church where Patience was working. That evening, as I settled into my seat, I saw Patience coming down my aisle. It had been several weeks since we had seen each other. When I asked the usual "how are you?" she responded by telling me that she was in a terrible amount of pain. She was working long hours on her feet, and her old prosthetic was wearing down and taking a toll on her body. She had met someone at church who referred her to a well-respected clinic in Athens, Georgia. She wept as she told me that she desperately knew she needed a new leg, but just out of college, things were a bit tight. I knew in my heart that I was being called to help her. Within a few days, things just seemed to work out in her favor, and Patience and I began weekly road trips for fitting appointments for a new prosthetic. I was incredibly blessed to be able to spend those days with such a sweet, kind, soft-spoken, and humble young lady. Thinking back to the very first time I saw her cheering from the stands, and that strong feeling I had in my heart to meet her, it is now so clear to me how God had orchestrated such an incredible divine appointment!

Over the course of the following year, Patience, Val, and I would begin to meet every month to reconnect and talk about how God was working in our lives. The blessings and gifts that God has given to them, they have shared with me. Their faith, determination, and positive attitudes have been true gifts to me. I have learned so much about life, faith, and love through these two genuine, caring, and God-fearing women.

Both Patience and Val's total reliance on God has never wavered, even in spite of their extremely difficult circumstances. They continue to have such a tremendous impact on the multitudes of people they have come into contact with, and I am just one of the fortunate ones to have had them woven into my life. When I think back to all the intricate details that became parts of those "woven threads," it is overwhelming. I do know that my actions were not orchestrated by me, but through God's prompting. I am so thankful that I was aware and obedient in seeing and responding to those little stirs in my heart that I refer to as nudges.

"Most people fail at whatever they attempt because of an undecided heart. Should I? Should I not? Go forward? Go back? Success requires the emotional balance of a committed heart. When confronted with a challenge, the committed heart will search for a solution. The undecided heart searches for an escape." (Andrews, The Traveler's Gift, 2002)

"Two people are better off than one,
for they can help each other succeed.
If one person falls, the other can
reach out and help. But someone
who falls alone is in real trouble.
Likewise, two people lying close
together can keep each other warm.
But how can one warm alone?
A person standing alone can be
attacked and defeated, but two can
stand back-to-back and conquer.
Three are even better, for a triple-
braided cord is not easily broken."
Ecclesiastes 4:9-12

God already knew what would happen to Val and He provided for her. Val is a woman of great strength and dignity and she lives her life to honor and glorify God. He aligned every minute detail in perfect timing to care for her. He knew she was a child of His, and He knew just who to send to help her accomplish His purpose. Like Val's story, we don't always have control over our circumstances, but we do have control over how we respond to, accept, and embrace our circumstances. HE works in us, through us and promises to equip us to accomplish His purpose.

None of us know what tomorrow holds or if we even have a tomorrow. Val's perspective is that her life is one of "unexpected interruptions," and God is using her to share her testimony of His unending love, mercy, and grace. She feels compelled to tell her story to the world so others can see how He has worked in and through her life. God has provided for her and is always faithful. Val has learned that suffering is not something we can avoid but something to embrace, and to learn and to grow from. She has embraced her new life with a tremendous sense of humor, amazing peace, and an everlasting joy.

"She is clothed in strength and dignity and laughs without fear of the future." When she speaks, her words are wise, and she gives instructions with kindness."
Proverbs 31:25-26

God is not in the punishing business; He is preparing you to trust His plan and not your pain. It's not the end of Val's story, but only the beginning. Her hope and strength, amidst so many difficult situations in her life, has prepared her to live out her story in order to inspire others. Val is a shining example of what it looks like to stand strong on both feet; to be bold with her faith; and to speak love and truth into the lives of others. That is her purpose and now her new platform.

She has had such an impact on my life, and I have no doubt that my life is more abundant and richer because of our friendship. To think it all started with a tap on my shoulder and a simple prayer. Val has taught me a lot about what genuine faith and love really are. She lives her life out in confidence, not as a disabled person but someone who has been made whole in her weakness. It is because of her disability that she has turned her suffering and pain into strength and can now reach out to a hurting and broken world to share the good news of Jesus and His saving grace. God knew all along the very people He was going to use to intercede, how and when it would happen. He had set it up from the very start with a tap on my shoulder. Our challenge is learning to listen to the quiet voice, and choosing to act on what we see, hear and feel. The catalyst started from an overwhelming stirring in my heart to meet an exuberant cheerleader who just happened to be an amputee, as well as a "chance meeting" with an airport employee with insight who offered prayer and words of encouragement to a complete stranger. Patience's zeal for life, Val's spiritual discernment, and the way God prepared and used me to be the conduit to weave the lives of the three of us intricately together, is nothing short of His divine plan. Over the course of time, I realized it wasn't just a few chance encounters, but saying YES to the little opportunities that come our way.

"What is always true is that decision that we make today determine the stories we tell about ourselves tomorrow. Every day, all day, we make one small choice after another. And those choices just keep accumulating, each one woven into the rest, forming the tapestry that is our life story" (Groeschel, 2016)

The story of Patience and Val are pretty awe-inspiring. It has opened my eyes in seeing how God works in the most intricate details of everyday life. Not every story is as dramatic as this one, but we can all find purpose in our daily encounters. Whether it is a simple smile or engaging someone in a conversation, we can all do our part to be a positive influence to those around us. I continually challenge myself to live consistent and authentic lives filled with truth, purpose, and perspective.

"The crisis of belief is a turning point where you must make a decision. You must decide. You must decide what you believe about God. How you respond at this turning point will determine whether you go on to be involved with God in something God-sized that only HE can do, or whether you will continue to go your own way and miss what God has purposed for your life" (Blackaby, Blackaby, and King, 2008).

"In the same way, let your good deeds shine out for all to see, so that everyone will praise your heavenly Father." Matthew 5:16

My Chance Encounters
HANGING ONTO HOPE

♡

*H*oday was another routine and normal day. Normal for me seems to involve running errands for our family and our business. I ran into a local store to purchase a travel journal for a client. As I reached the back of the store two women were standing in front of the large selection journals. As I began looking through the journals, I smiled and made eye contact with the two women. I had found the perfect travel journal with a world map on the front cover. But it seemed I was drawn to another navy blue journal as well. It had an anchor on it with the word HOPE inscribed on the front. As I took the journal in my hand, one of the women commented on the beautiful journal. Hope; something my youngest son so desperately needed. He had been suffering with chronic pain in his neck and excess of five long years, traipsing from one doctor to another searching for answers. More than five specialists, many epidural injections, two pain management doctors, physical therapy, chiropractic care, massage therapy, acupuncture, and still no relief from his pain. I mentioned to the two ladies I was going to buy the journal with the anchor on it for my son, hoping it would provide him with some much-needed encouragement. I mentioned he had a doctor's appointment the following day. In the blink of an eye, they asked if they could pray with me right in the middle of the store. I wept as I joined hands in prayer with two complete strangers, who boldly asked God for healing for my son. As it turns out, these women were mother and daughter, the daughter a pastor. They were merely passing through town and decided on a whim to go shopping. Obviously, at that very moment, they felt that familiar prompting from God and chose to be bold and obedient. Once again, God sent me to that very place and had set up another incredible divine appointment.

"I want them to be encouraged and knit together by strong ties of love. I want them to have complete confidence that they understand GODS mysterious plan, which is Christ himself." Colossians 2:2

THE SURPRISE CALL

*a*s I stood in line at our local Wal-Mart store, I smiled and said "hello" to the woman in front of me. She was busy trying to corral two young children who I surmised were perhaps her grandchildren. As she finished up paying for her groceries, I asked her to wait just a minute. I felt that familiar tug at my heart and dashed back and grabbed another devotional book off the shelf. The cashier rang up my order and after inscribing my name and phone number in the front of the book, I handed it to this stranger. Over the last seven years since our "chance" meeting, I really hadn't given much more thought about that random gesture. Until one day my phone rang. Usually when a name doesn't pre-populate on my phone, I let the call go to voicemail. Not this time. The woman's voice at the other end of the phone introduced herself as Diana. She told me she was the woman I had given the devotional book to at Wal-Mart seven years ago. She wanted to call me to let me know how God had been working in her life since the day I gave her the book. Her daughter had run off and left her to raise her two grandchildren and Diana had been in school, trying to restart her dream to become a nurse. She ended up having to quit school to take care of the girls. But with no job and no money, they were living out of her car and eating from a cooler she kept in the back seat. She proceeded to tell me how much she had treasured the little devotional book she had kept in her purse all those years. She read it over and over, claiming the promises it held inside its pages. God's promise to never leave her or abandon her. Then one day, she "coincidentally" met a man who God would use to help her financially: giving her a roof over her head and eventually helping her through nursing school. As she spoke, tears of joy fell from my eyes. I wept as this total stranger from a random meeting seven years earlier in a Wal-Mart store, shared with me just how God pulled her up out of a place of hopelessness to a life filled with meaning and purpose. Today, her grandchildren have been reunited with their mother, and Diana is a registered nurse on a cancer ward in a neighboring county.

God is good. He does provide, and sometimes it is in the smallest gestures of kindness that He chooses to use us. I am so humbled and thankful Diana called me that day, seven years later, to tell me of God's incredible love and faithfulness. Had she not, I would never have known how one simple act of kindness can touch another person's life. Once again, I was truly overwhelmed at God's provision and His perfect timing.

"So be strong and courageous! Do not be afraid and do not panic before them. For the Lord your God will personally go ahead of you. He will neither fail you nor abandon you." Deuteronomy 31:6

THE ANSWERED PRAYER

*H*he date had been set for our church's community-wide women's event. I had volunteered to secure a couple of door prizes for this quarterly gathering for the women in our county. Several weeks prior to the actual event, I had secured a couple of items but needed one more. I knew the owner of the nail salon just around the corner from our church, so I decided to drop by one day to ask if she would be willing to donate a gift certificate. She was extremely busy that day, so I offered to come back the week prior to the event. The morning of the event, I was at our church helping to coordinate some last-minute things for the evening, and I thought I would run over to the nail salon.

When I walked in the door the owner greeted me and without hesitation, she said she would be happy to provide not one, but two gift certificates for our event. Finishing up the gift certificates, she paused, and asked me to pray for a friend. She went on to tell me her friend was expecting a baby, and the doctor had planned to take the baby early. As she handed me the certificates, I thanked her and promised I would pray for her friend and her unborn child. Once again, I felt that familiar tug in my heart. I reached slowly into my purse for the packet of scripture cards I always carry with me. As she read the one she had chosen a tear began to fall upon her cheek. Welled up with emotion, she handed me the card and it read: "For you created my inmost being, you knit me together in my mother's womb. I praise you because I am fearfully and wonderfully made" (Psalm 139: 13,14).

My eyes welled up and I was overcome with tears of joy at God's divine appointment, His timing of my steps and just the right scripture for my friend. As I drove back to the church, I was overcome with emotion of what had just happened. I gathered the other ladies around me and told them of my experience at the nail salon. We formed a circle and prayed for the mother and her unborn baby. I was supposed to have gone to pick up the gift certificate the week before, but God had other plans for me. My plans may have been diverted, but God 's plans never are. I have since found out God did indeed answer our prayers that day; both Mom and her new baby are both healthy and thriving!

"You can make many plans, but the LORDS purpose will prevail."
Proverbs 19:21

LIFE IS ABOUT THE PEOPLE,
NOT THE PLACE

ince 2006, Roatan, Honduras has become a very special place to our family. We have so many wonderful memories of our time spent there with family and friends. Every trip brings with it a new adventure and the opportunity to experience life from a new and different cultural perspective. Roatan, one of The Bay Islands, is a little gem located off the coast of the mainland of Honduras. With its crystal blue turquoise water and second largest reef in the world, the marine life is spectacular. There are a multitude of activities from zip lining, to diving, snorkeling and swimming with the dolphins. A trip to Roatan wouldn't be complete until you've also had a chance to visit Arch's Iguana Farm. What draws me back to this beautiful place, time and time again are the people. We have been fortunate to have the opportunity to meet so many special people, such as the Arch family, who have opened their hearts and home to us over the years. We will always treasure the connections we have made that make this island so special. Another special friend I always look forward to seeing in this tropical paradise is Francis.

With the water gently lapping onto the sandy beach, I sat watching her walking barefoot toward me, balancing her heavy massage table on her head. As I said, "Good morning," she smiled a wide smile, her beautiful, brown

Honduran skin glistening in the early morning sun. I watched as she set up her table and umbrella for the day about a hundred yards down the beach from where I had found a comfortable, shady spot underneath several coconut palms. My attention was deep into my novel, but there was something about her smile that tugged at my heart. I decided to walk down the beach and introduce myself to this woman I was drawn to. In broken English, she told me her name was Francis. I speak very little Spanish; in fact, I only know a few of the simple and common phrases and words like Hola, Buenos Dias and bano. Thankfully, another beach vendor was stationed very close to Francis. He could hear that we were trying to converse and kindly walked over to where we were to interpret for us.

Born on the island of Roatán, Francis worked incredibly long, hours in the hot sun every day to support her young family. Most of the beach vendors walk up and down the beach bargaining with the many tourists. Not Francis. With her soft-spoken and meek disposition, it seems her clients always found her under the shade of her umbrella.

One March to celebrate my birthday, we invited some friends to join us and to experience the beautiful island of Roatan and its people. Anxious to see the beach, the first morning my friends and I headed out for a walk down to where Francis had her massage table set up. My heart kept telling me that there was something unique and special about this lady. My friend went on to tell Francis we were there on vacation and I would be celebrating my birthday the next day. The next morning one of my friends insisted we all go for a walk down the beach. Not fifty yards away, with her massage table tucked up under a tree, stood Francis. She smiled and motioned for us to come over. As we walked toward her, I looked down and could see she had drawn a heart in the sand and outlined it with beautiful flower petals. In the center of the heart, it read, "Happy Birthday Mare." On her massage table sat a beautiful birthday cake just for me. I was overcome with emotion as my new friend hugged me, wishing me a happy birthday. Francis may not have much in the way material possessions, but her kindness and thoughtfulness touched me and spoke volumes to me of her character.

On the second-to-last day of our trip, my friend sprained her ankle. Each evening, we would head down to the beach to sit and watch the beautiful sunset that God had painted for us. Susan was sitting with her swollen and throbbing ankle wrapped up when along came Francis, her massage table on her head. As she made her way over to where we were sitting, she could see Susan was hurting. Without hesitation, and unable to speak our language, she immediately began to prop Susan's leg up. She found a sand bucket and filled it with water, ran to a nearby restaurant and filled the bucket with ice, bringing it back to ice down Susan's injured ankle. It was so heart-warming to see her care for Susan, a stranger. Her love and unselfish compassion to help a complete stranger was such a blessing to witness.

For over a decade, we have made the journey to Roatan a few times a year, and I would not have to look too far down the beach to find my friend Francis. She would have her massage table set up just a few yards away from the shore of the crystal-clear Caribbean water. Not only would I get the best $25 hour massage on the beach, Francis and I, with all our differences in language and culture, had cultivated an undeniable and wonderful friendship. I think back to the first time I met her, with her kind smile and warm brown eyes. I will always remember the time I asked her to speak to me in Spanish about the island. I recorded her in order to share the recording with a local public school our business had partnered with back in the U.S.

Earlier in that week, she had asked how she could pray for me. I told her a little bit of what I had been struggling with. Sitting on a beach chair and looking out over the turquoise Caribbean water, she began quickly speaking in her native tongue. I had no idea what she was saying but at one point, a tear began to fall from her cheek. As the tears began to slowly roll down her cheeks, she would simultaneously touch her hand to her heart and point to the sky. She spoke nonstop and passionately for over ten minutes. Once she finished speaking, we embraced, and I offered up my heart-felt "Gracias."

Upon arriving home, I emailed a friend the video I had taken of Francis to have her translate it into English for me. My first thought was that perhaps something had gotten lost in the translation. As I sat down at my computer and began to read the translation, I began to cry. Her video was not about the island, but with passion in her voice, she was actually praying for my family and me. It was so apparent that Francis was a genuine and sincere person with a heart for others. She has always reflected and shined the light of God's love. Once again, I was in awe that God had provided a stranger to pray for me.

On another trip down, Francis told me she was a Sunday school teacher. I asked her if there was anything I could bring back for their church. Knowing many children on this island have very little compared to our standards, I was anxious to help. When I arrived the following December with a suitcase full of crayons and coloring books, the children were so excited and very appreciative to have just ONE crayon to color with! It was such a blessing for me to see the smiles on the children's faces. They were so happy to receive the things we would consider so little. Over the past several years, we have had the privilege of meeting Francis's pastor and with assistance from family and friends have been able to continue to bless the children of her church.

On one of my most recent trips to the island, Francis had shared with me that she hadn't seen her mother in seventeen years, who lives in Austin, Texas The next day, I ran into a couple from Roatan we had become friends with over the years. In passing, they mentioned they had friends originally from the mainland visiting Roatan from of all places, Austin, Texas. My mind was whizzing as I thought maybe, just maybe, God was using me at this very moment, orchestrating this series of events, to help Frances reconnect with her mother in Austin. I told my friend about Francis and her desire to connect with her mother. Later that very afternoon, as I was walking toward the beach, my friend approached me and wanted to introduce her friends from Austin to me. After a few brief minutes of introductions and small talk, I shared with them my friendship with Francis. As we continued talking, we strolled down the beach to where Francis's massage table was set up. I introduced my new friends to Francis and they immediately broke into Spanish, hugging each other. It was an instant connection, perhaps a divine appointment. On the last day of our trip, I ran into my new friends from Austin on the beach. The lady told me she had spoken to Francis several times during the week and promised Francis that when she returned to home, she planned to meet up with Francis's mom.

To this day, I do not know if the connection happened, but what I do know is that in God's timing, Francis and her mother will be reunited. We must trust that God is working in and through us, and trust that in His timing, He will see it through.

What have made our visits to this beautiful island so special are the beautiful people and friendships we have made along the way. I have always said, "It's the people that make the place, not the place that makes the people!" I came to the realization that day just exactly why. When I first met Francis, I had an overwhelming feeling that she was a unique and compassionate person. Her love for God and people is so outwardly apparent. I witnessed firsthand she is a child of God and how much she loves Him wholeheartedly. She lives for God, sharing love and joy by serving and helping others every day. Francis may not have an abundance of material things, but she has the abundant love of her Heavenly Father, something that cannot be purchased.

"And this same GOD who takes care of me will supply all your needs from his glorious riches, which have been given to us in Christ Jesus."

Philippians 4:19

OUR PURPOSE,
GOD'S PLAN

♡

*E*very so often, I go and treat myself to a pedicure. When I do, I usually frequent the same nail salon. I was rushing around, trying to get ready to leave town for a wedding. It just so happened to be the wedding of my dear friend, Patience! I sat down at the table and a sweet, young Vietnamese girl greeted me and motioned for me to sit across the table from her. Her beautiful, brown eyes reflected kindness, and I could see the corners of her wide smile rising from the sides of the surgical mask she was wearing. She spoke English well, asking me how I wanted my nails done. Our conversation was easy, as I asked her about her family, to which she told me she had five children. It was at this point in our conversation that I felt that nudge, that little something prompting my heart. We talked of today's sad reality our children are being raised in a world of excessive technology, less human interaction and fewer relationships with God and people. With a tear beginning to fall from the corner of her eye and down her cheek, she went on to tell me that she knows the one true God. I told her I knew it wasn't mere " chance" that she was doing my nails. She went on to tell me that it wasn't even her turn to do my nails, and there were three other employees ahead of her on the rotation, but we both knew it was God who "set up" my nail appointment that day. I asked her if she was familiar with the scripture Romans 8:28. With tears streaming down her face, she took out her phone as she read the verse out loud. "And we know that all things work together for good to those who love God, to those who are called according to His purpose." When I left the nail salon that day, I too had tears streaming down my cheeks: reflecting on the goodness of God, His incredible timing, and the way He can use even a manicure appointment and a young, Vietnamese nail technician to spread His love in a world that so desperately needs it.

THE FABRIC OF FRIENDSHIP

♡

"Friendship is the golden thread that ties the heart of all the world" (John Evelyn, goodreads.com).

hroughout my life, I have been extremely blessed with so many wonderful, kind, loyal, and faithful friends who have walked along side me. Living so far away from family, the friends God has placed in my path have been there for me during the inevitable peaks and valleys that accompany life. From the birth of children, grandchildren, to weddings, college graduations, surgeries, and sicknesses, they were there.

Over the years and moving to new places, I knew it was imperative that I put myself out there and meet new people. Each move we have made has provided our family the opportunity to develop so many wonderful, lasting friendships. These friendships have woven some of the most beautiful threads into my life's tapestry. I believe God never makes a mistake. He is constantly intervening in our lives, speaking to us in different ways and at different times so that we may know He is the very author of our appointments and disappointments. We may not fully grasp His design as it takes shape, but we need to trust that He has a plan and a purpose for everything. His plans are never diverted, and He is the master weaver! Like the game of chess, and with each piece on the board strategically positioned, God is always preparing us for our next move, aligning things for our next divine appointment. I have grown to realize that if we are obedient, our hearts will guide us and help us notice and recognize these opportunities, "appointments" when they occur. God will never ask us to do anything He will not equip us to do. I have such love and respect for the many special people God has placed in my path, from my parents who gave me a strong moral compass, to my husband, my children, my family, my siblings and my friends. To those friends and family not mentioned in this book, you have woven countless beautiful threads into my life.

I know for certain God has placed each one of you in my life for a reason, some for a season and others for a lifetime.

"For everything there is a season, a time for every activity under heaven." Ecclesiastes 3:1

ONE MAN'S TRASH,
ANOTHER MAN'S TREASURE

♡

"Dear brothers and sisters, when troubles of any kind come your way, it is an opportunity for great joy. For you know that when your faith is tested, your endurance has a chance to grow. So let it grow, for when your endurance is fully developed, you will be perfect and complete, needing nothing."

James 1:2-4

I love to walk. I especially love to walk in our neighborhood with its meandering sidewalks where you can walk for miles and miles. One cool spring afternoon, I took my standard route. Only a few houses away from home, I "just happened" to walk by as one of my neighbors was rolling her trash bin out to the curb for pick up. I felt that strong inclination, that nudge to speak to this person and engage her in conversation. We had never met, so I said hello and introduced myself. Sharon's warm and friendly personality made our conversation effortless. She had just moved into the neighborhood a few months prior. The longer we spoke, the more we realized we had a lot in common. We stood beside her trash bin talking for over an hour. She mentioned she loved to walk too, so we exchanged phone numbers and I went on my way. Over the course of the next few weeks and months we would meet up every couple of days to walk. Naturally, while we were walking, we also did a lot of talking. As our friendship grew, we began sharing the details of our lives with each other. At this point in my life, I was deeply burdened for Steven, our youngest son. I shared the health struggles he was going through with Sharon. She kindly offered to pray for wisdom, direction and answers for his declining health. She then opened up to me about the long and difficult journey she had with her own health issues.

We had been hitting dead ends with Steven, with countless number of doctor's visits over the course of many months. Sharon could relate to the frustration we were facing. Since we weren't making any progress and Steven's symptoms were worsening, Sharon recommended we see the doctor who helped uncover her illness. At our very first appointment, her doctor spent over two hours with us, listening, analyzing and discussing Steven's symptoms with he and I. Leaving her office that day, we were hopeful. The doctor ordered a multitude of different tests for further investigation. For the first time in months we felt that perhaps we had found the person who was going to dig and get to the bottom of Steven's health problem. I began wracking my brain to think of what had changed with Steven when his health began to decline. Sharon suggested we have his living environment checked. Not a week later, I received a text message from Sharon, with the contact information to another doctor, a specialist she had heard about through a friend. I did some research and called and made an appointment for Steven. I truly believe that God was at work; from the very moment I met Sharon. I am absolutely certain He was guiding every step of my walk that day, leading us down a path that could lead to a diagnosis and healing for Steven. Over the course of many months, with Steven's health declining we were fortunate to have had many wonderful friends and family fervently praying for the healing of his body, mind and spirit. As his parents, we would continue to pray, listen to that still small voice and trust that God would continue to guide us and give us direction. I have witnessed Steven's unwavering faith through this journey. I can look back and see how his years of spiritual growth have been an integral part God's plan for Steven to know Him, trust Him and to lean on Him during these long and challenging months. He poured his heart and soul into reading scripture, soaking in God's promises and leaning on Him as his rock and protector during this trying time in his life. As I reflect back over the course of time, I knew deep in my heart that Steven was ill. Early on I had vowed to Steven (as any mother would), that he could depend on me to help him fight through this challenge and that we as a family would be there for him every step of the way. One of the hardest things to watch as a parent has been the emotional toll this has been on my son. Time lost, money spent, dead ends and no answers. Only medications offered to treat a multitude of symptoms, without a clear direction in finding the root cause of his sickness. That is, until I met Sharon. I know without a doubt God placed her along my walk that day to be the conduit to help Steven get on the path to wellness and recovery. Sharon's very similar personal health struggle gave us confirmation, encouragement and hope to understand that God is in control and He is at the center of bringing restoration and healing. Sharon's wisdom, guidance, heartfelt advice and genuine love and concern are something I will always treasure and be grateful for.

I cannot wait to see how God will use Steven to share the news of His goodness and provision through this difficult time in his life. I know God has a plan and a purpose for him! I have no doubt when Steven fully recovers as a healthy young man, he will be able to use his journey through this experience to be the encouragement for someone else. Who would have ever imagined that someone simply taking out her trash would be the answer to our prayers for Steven's healing? Only God. What a treasure!!

"The LORD is my rock, my fortress, and my savior; my God is my rock in whom I find protection. He is my shield, the power that saves me, and my place of safety."
Psalm 18:2

LOVE WINS

"*Pain is inevitable, but misery is optional. We cannot avoid pain, but we can avoid joy.*" *Tim Hansel (goodreads.com)*

If you're like me, we have all had times in our lives when we have found ourselves in a valley. How do you respond in the valley? How do you handle the suffering and pain that comes your way, the times when you feel overwhelmed with worry, and your heart aches with sadness? I have lived through such a time as this, where I have fervently prayed, pleading and wrestling with God to change a certain situation. My prayer was for healing and for God to intervene in the life of someone I dearly love. I felt certain He was not calling me to be that someone to intercede. But, in fact, He was. He answered my prayers by sending some wise and discerning friends my way. He was shaping me and teaching me to show love. How we react when we are tested reveals our heart. James 1: 2-4 says that it is in those tough times our faith is tested and shows its true colors. I must admit, during this time, I undoubtedly showed my true colors. And they were not pretty colors. My emotions would run high with disappointment and anger would boil inside of me. But I knew deep down that I would never give up on praying for this person I loved so dearly. I knew God would never give up on her, so why should I? I guess that's what happens when we love and care for someone so deeply. I pray out of love and I know prayer has the power to change lives. There is no pretending or hiding when addiction ravages your family, someone we love passes away, your business struggles or your kids mess up. But the good news is God provides hope. He did it for me and He will do it for you. Looking back, I can clearly see what God was up to. He was convicting me and growing me in my faith. Teaching me to learn to depend on Him, to be kind and share His love, hope and encouragement in a very challenging situation. We have the opportunity to be the light in the darkness for those who so desperately need His love, mercy and grace. I spent many sleepless nights, tossing and turning, unable to shut my mind off. My stress was causing my health to suffer. But it was out of my struggle, my valley, that so many hidden blessings were revealed. (Val tapping my shoulder in the airport that day.) Throughout this time, sweet friendships were nurtured and developed; friends with listening ears and prayerful hearts, friends who had walked the road I was on and could relate to what I was going through. They gave me spiritual guidance, invaluable wisdom, and unconditional love throughout this journey. I also learned so much about myself. I have learned how the giving and receiving of love can heal and mend those broken and frayed stitches, restoring them and weaving them into something beautiful. My heart needed to soften, and I needed to learn to forgive and to reflect love. With harsh, but powerful words, (and a bit of a lecture) one dear friend boldly told me to "LOVE anyway." Love can and will restore broken, shattered relationships. Love does win. Love is not dependent upon our circumstances. It is in our circumstances we learn how to forgive and to love. It was in this valley that God taught me how a fervent, unshakable faith leads to joy. Both joy and sorrow are inevitable and are intricately interwoven. Joy is not a warm, fuzzy feeling, but a conviction. Joy is rooted in seeds of gratitude. We cannot live a life of joy with an ungrateful heart. Throughout our lives, God knits and weaves together the fragments of both our painful and joyful experiences. Joy is truly God's purpose for your life. (Romans 8:28) Reflect on your blessings, live in the moment, and decrease your stress to find the blessings in your mess. It will become your message. As Kay Warren states in her book *Choose Joy*, "Joy is the settled assurance that God is in control of all of the details of my life, the quiet confidence that ultimately everything is going to be alright, and the determined choice to praise God in all things" (2012). I challenge you to tape it to your mirror, memorize it and CHOOSE joy.

"Love is patient and kind. Love is not jealous or boastful or proud."
1 Corinthians 13:4

MY WOVEN TAPESTRY

Susan

*L*ooking back over our forty-six years of friendship, it is truly remarkable that two little 6th grade girls would continue to nurture an incredible relationship over their lifetimes. Susan and I have walked through many of life's ups and downs together; from weddings (our own and our children's), to childbirth, to grandchildren, health issues, and family challenges. There has never been a moment when I called her that she wasn't there to listen. The memories and shared history we have as 12-year-old little girls and through our adult lives are truly unique and incredibly special.

Veronica

During our first year of marriage in "the Land Down Under," and so far away from family, God truly sent a friend named Veronica to help guide me as a young newlywed. Moving back to the U.S. from South Australia all those years ago I had lost touch with Veronica. For years, I had thought about her and had tried all I knew to get in touch with her, but to no avail. Thirty-two years later, we planned a trip back to Australia where my marriage first took flight. It was on this trip where I felt the prompting once again to try to find my old friend. That prompting was so strong while in Sydney, so I decided to check the White Pages. What chance could there be that Veronica had moved from South Australia to the state of New South Wales, over 1,500 miles away? Low and behold, I had found her husband's name and address but no phone number. It was our last day in the beautiful city of Sydney, and I was determined to find some way to reach her. I ran down to the souvenir shop and purchased a postcard. I addressed it to Veronica, along with a short note and my email address. I stuck it in the mail the very morning we were flying back to the US. Incredibly, upon arriving home, I opened my email and there was a message from Veronica. I was so glad I had persisted in trying to locate my old friend and mentor. It had been over thirty-two years since we had communicated. At last we had reconnected!

Laurie

Fast-forward twenty-eight years. It was the fall of 2018, and Mitchell and I made plans to go to Fayetteville, Arkansas to a Razorback football game. Our boys had both graduated, but we decided to take in one game that Fall. We filed into our seats at midfield just in time for the National Anthem. Just a few minutes into the game, I glanced at the group of women sitting directly in front of us who were laughing and chatting. I caught a glimpse of the profile of the blonde girl sitting in front and to the left of me, and low and behold, it was Laurie, my old friend and neighbor from so many years ago. I leaned forward and tapped her on the shoulder. As she turned around, she screamed the moment our eyes met. We hugged for what seemed an eternity. How could it be that my long-lost friend from so many years ago "just happened" to be sitting in front of me in a stadium field with over 70,000 people? Perhaps God was once again up to something.

Rhonda

Thirty-four years ago, and to think my neighbor would talk to a random stranger in the airport and that random stranger, who lived several states away, would become a very dear friend and spiritual mentor. Rhonda poured the love of Jesus into my opening heart all those years ago and helped the Lord align my heart and mind to His purpose for my life. She has been there to both encourage me to write this book and through the editing process. I have no doubt that only God could have orchestrated this divine appointment all those years ago.

Val

It is truly remarkable how God weaves people into our lives; some to stay just a little while, and others for a lifetime. Val and I continue to get together periodically for dinner to catch up on what's going on in our lives. She has the undeniable knack for discerning what is happening in my life and continues to give me spiritual guidance. The pearls of wisdom she imparts, and her discerning spirit has taught me so much. She challenges me to love others well, even those who at times can be unlovable. She continually reminds me of who God is and how fulfilling our lives can be when we trust Him. She continues to know just the right time to send me an encouraging text message, always signing off with her signature saying, "Love you more!" I will always treasure her friendship and thank God He has woven her into my life. She speaks the truth from her heart and encourages me to live out my faith. And coming from someone who has faced so many obstacles along the way, she continues to challenge me to always choose joy in my journey.

Patience

Currently, Patience is living out God's calling on her life in a ministry position at a church out West. It was at this church where she recently met and married the man of her dreams. She has developed a passion for snowboarding and, in her spare time, heads to the nearest mountain. She has set her sights on the next Paralympics.

I miss her so much but know that God has her exactly where He wants her. We talk often, pray for each other, and have a bond that will last a lifetime.

Mrs. Hermecz

About two years ago, I received a phone call. Nothing came up on my caller ID, but I answered it anyway. The voice on the end of the phone sounded so very familiar; it was

Mrs. Hermecz, our son's second-grade teacher. She went on to tell me that the reason she was calling was she had been thinking about our family. She actually expressed that God had been waking her up in the middle of the night with our family on her mind. That is when she was prompted to call me. She asked if everything was OK, to which I replied that we had been going through a challenging season with our business. She then asked me if I would like to get together for lunch one day soon. We picked a day and met the following week. Over lunch, we caught up on our lives, the lives of our children, and our jobs. Of course, since she and Steven shared a special bond, she was anxious to know about him. She then asked me about my life, curious to know what I had been doing. It was then I told her I was feeling called to write a book about "divine appointments." I went on to tell her that I was stuck and was not making progress with my writing. It was at that very moment she told me she smiled and told me she wanted me to meet a friend of hers; a young girl who had just published her own book. She gave me Lauren's number and insisted I call her. Over the course of the last year, Lauren has given me such encouragement and helped me navigate through the book-writing and publishing process.

Who would have thought that Steven's second grade teacher would be just the person to introduce me to someone that could help me fulfill my dream of writing this book?

Mitchell

After thirty-six years of marriage, I have been fortunate enough to still be married to the man of my dreams, my best friend. All those years ago, God placed Mitchell in that restaurant at just the right time. How very different my life's journey would be if we had never met. His very character and unwavering faith have helped me become who I am today. We've raised two incredible children, built a business together, and have survived many of life's ups and downs, always keeping God at the center of our lives. I am so thankful for his encouragement and the countless hours of editing this book. I am truly blessed.

Conclusion

OPEN EYES, OPEN HEART

eading my story, I hope you will be encouraged; encouraged to step out of your comfort zone and open your eyes and heart to embrace and act upon the opportunities God places in front of you. Let God use your story, your triumphs, and your victories, as well as your defeats and your failures, to encourage others on their life journey. We all have the power to speak life into others through our encouraging words and kind actions. Oftentimes, when we are going through the valleys of life; illnesses, death, financial burdens, challenging people, and situations, we cannot see how God is working. Your hurts, your disappointments can mold your heart to be bitter, broken, or tender. In this life, it is certain we will all experience joy and pain. If you open your heart, mind, and soul to God, He will carry you through both the joyful and painful, times of life. God can and will use both our joy and our heartaches to accomplish His purpose and fulfill His plans for our lives. He understands our deepest pain and disappointments. We sometimes wonder why God isn't changing our circumstances. Oftentimes, He is concerned about changing YOU and NOT your circumstances. It is in the hard moments our faith is tested. How we respond in those moments is where God meets us. The knotted underside of your tapestry, with all of its tangled and jumbled mess of threads, represents those valleys. Looking back over the course of months and even years, we are able to see the beautiful design He has created, tying both the tangled, jumbled and colorful threads together that He has woven throughout our lives. It is only when we turn our tapestry over and marvel at the front side, we can see its beauty. God created you; your DNA is unique and special, and He has a plan and purpose for your life. From experience, if you will begin to notice others, God will begin to work in and through you in ways you could never imagine. Learn how to love both God and the very people He has put around you. The threads of your hopes, dreams and your calling will all fall into place and will honor and glorify God.

Have faith in knowing God will work all things together for your good, and trust that His timing is perfect. Everything you do matters to God: your character, your inner strength, and your integrity. They matter because they are everlasting qualities. The wisdom and the maturity that grows within you from your experiences are what will help define the purpose God has for you. Simply pray and ask God to reveal your purpose and you will find a life of value and significance. God hears our prayers and is in every single detail of our lives.

On my journey I have learned to slow down, to be more intentional in my actions, and to be more aware of the people He has placed in my path. You might just be a blessing to someone else!

"Dear children, let's not merely say we love each other; let us show the truth by our actions." 1 John 3:18

As I finish writing this book, our world is in the midst of the Covid-19 pandemic. I do not believe this is a coincidence: God is speaking to us in these uncertain times to learn to rely on Him and to remind us that He is in control. Perhaps He is drawing us to Him to make us aware of the many distractions so that we can focus on Him and the true purpose and meaning for our lives. Reach out and begin a relationship with Him. Open your heart and learn to see how much God really loves you. He will change your life for all of eternity. He will be your strength and confidant in troubled times and your greatest encourager during good times. God is always faithful, and available to you. He longs to empower you and use you in unimaginable ways: to share His promises, mercy and grace, love, and peace to a desperate and hurting world.

"Dont be afraid, for I am with you. Dont be discouraged, for I am your GOD. I will strengthen you and help you. I will hold you up with my victorious right hand."

Isaiah 41:10

When I think back over my life, I am in awe of the many times I have been touched and prompted by God, and I have no doubt they were not mere coincidences. God has used me, a small-town girl from Ontario, Canada, to be His vessel to show others His love, power, mercy, and grace. The divine appointments I have experienced have been nothing short of amazing and miraculous, and I truly believe no one other than God has orchestrated them. Had I not said "yes" to marrying the man of my dreams, or to Val's simple yet profound prayer in the airport that day, my life's experiences, and journey would be so very different. More importantly, I would have missed out on the blessings placed in front of me. I am grateful God has been watching over me, guiding me, directing me, and had a plan and purpose for my life from the day I was born.

"You made all of the delicate, inner parts of my body and knit me together in my mother's womb. Thank you for making me so wonderfully complex! Your workmanship is marvelous— how well I know it. You watched me as I was being formed in utter seclusion, as I was woven together in the dark of the womb. You saw me before I was born. Every day of my life was recorded in your book. Every moment was laid out before a single day had passed."

Psalm 139:13-16

"Tree of Life"
"Foundation Stones of Life?"

- BE FISCALLY RESPONSIBLE - (POP IS AN EXPERIENCED PERSON
                                      IN THIS CATEGORY)
- RESPECT ELDERS   (JOKE)
- LEARNING & GROWING
- COMMUNITY SERVICE
- TEMPERANCE (DRINKING & GAMBLING)
- BE HAPPY - HAVE SENSE OF HUMOUR
- GOOD MORALS
- HEALTHY ATTITUDE
  TOWARD RACE OF PEOPLE + TOLERANCE
- SMILE
- BE A ROLE MODEL FOR CHILDREN
- GOOD
  LANGUAGE
- GET AN EDUCATION
- CONTROL TEMPER BUT
- BE COMPETITIVE.
- NICE MANNERS.

- SPIRITUALITY:
- GO TO CHURCH
- EXERCISE REGULARLY
- EAT WISELY
- MAKE WISE DECISIONS
  THROUGH LIFE
         AND FINALLY:
- DON'T PICK YOUR NOSE!

FIRM ROOTS
SOLID FOUNDATION

"I'd rather have Jesus, than silver or gold"
Author unknown

MR. HICKS
PRESIDENT   PRECIOUS   MIKE   STEVO   "PEACHIE"

ACKNOWLEDGEMENTS

Not only has God placed amazing people in my path and provided purpose in my journey, He has strategically provided the people to help me fulfill my desire to share my stories. Who would have thought that God would prompt my youngest son's teacher from over twenty years ago to call me? And even more remarkable, that she would know just the right person to help my book become a reality. Lauren has been there to edit and encourage me to get this project to completion. We have developed a sweet friendship and for that, I will be forever grateful.

"The heartfelt counsel of a friend is as sweet as perfume and incense."
Proverbs 27:9

Everyone has stories about how they met, especially all the chance encounters and unexpected introductions. It was an impromptu invitation to an event from a mutual friend where I met Cynthia. Our conversation was natural, and I was immediately drawn to her warm and witty personality. Little did I know that several months later, she would be one of the several people that said "yes" to helping me write this book. Without Cynthia, not one word would have been written on these pages. She encouraged me to begin and steadfastly stood by me during the many edits and changes it takes for a book to come to fruition.

In the words of Minx Boren, "Friends are the patient gardeners who, year after year encourage our souls to blossom" (2016).

On a recent trip, I will never forget Rhonda and her husband asking me if I had a dream. That was five years ago, and my answer was "No, not really." There were places in this world that I dreamed to visit, but I didn't have a deep, driving sense of having to accomplish something significant, other than being a devoted wife, loving mother and grandmother, and the CEO (chief encouragement officer) of our family-owned business.

As I look back over this book, which is a story of my own woven threads, I am in awe. Rhonda has been there for me, to guide me, edit for me; and for her, I am truly grateful!

To say God put the dream of writing this book in my heart is an understatement!

"There are "friends" who destroy each other, but a real friend sticks closer than a brother."
Proverbs 18:24

Having been a part of a global travel franchise for over thirty years has not only allowed our family the benefit of international travel but gave me the opportunity to meet many wonderful and special people along the way. From the founder of our franchise, his wife and family, to the other franchisees, we have been so blessed to develop many deep and lasting business and personal relationships. Julie, a franchisee's wife I met over seven years ago, has become a special friend. Recently, while scrolling through Instagram, I came across one of Julie's creative posts. It just so happened it was at the very time I was trying to come up with a visual for my book's cover. Her timely post was a piece of beautiful needlework she had just created. It was exactly what I had been visualizing and had in mind for my book's cover. Once again, God provided just who I needed to complete this project. Julie, with her God-given, artistic ability, graciously offered to create the beautiful cover for this book.

"I tell you, you can pray for anything, and if you believe that you have received it, it will be yours." Mark 11:24

As I look back on my childhood, I am so grateful for my parents for instilling Christian morals and values into my life. My mother, the most selfless and thoughtful and caring human I know, would write me little notes of encouragement, and tuck them under my pillow or in my lunch bag. She would scribble this Bible verse on a little piece of paper or in a card: 1 Corinthians 13:13: "And, now these three remain; faith, hope and love, but the greatest of these is love." Yes, love conquers all. My father, a sentimental and thoughtful man has a huge heart. After marrying and moving away from home at the age of 22, I will forever cherish all those handwritten letters and notes of encouragement, with their heart felt words and hand-drawn caricatures. And when I say letters, I mean I have shoeboxes full of them. I thank God for my parents and my siblings for the love they continually and unconditionally give, the wisdom they share, and the sacrifices they have made for my family and me.

While reading through this book, my hope and prayer is that you will begin to see the threads the Lord has graciously and incredibly woven into my life; and that you would be inspired and encouraged to become more aware of the opportunities to shine the light of God and share His love and hope with those around you.

"In the same way, let your good deeds shine out for all to see, so that everyone will praise your heavenly Father." Matthew 5:16

BIBLIOGRAPHY

Andrews, Andy, *The Noticer*. Nashville, Tennessee: Thomas Nelson, 2009.

Andrews, Andy, *The Traveler's Gift—Seven Decisions that Determine Personal Success*. Nashville, Tennessee: Thomas Nelson, 2002.

Andrews, Andy, *The Butterfly Effect*. Nashville, Tennessee: Thomas Nelson 2010.

Blackaby, Henry; Blackaby, Richard, and King, Claude, *Experiencing God-Knowing and Doing*

The Will of God. Nashville, Tennessee. B and H Publishing Group, 2008.

Boren, Minix, *Friendship is a Journey- A Celebration of True Connection and Deep Caring*, Boulder, Colorado: Blue Mountain Arts, Inc. 2016.

Everlyn, John. "Friendship is the golden thread that ties the heart of all the world" (quote). Goodreads website, Accessed June 15, 2020, www.goodreads.com.

Groeschel, Craig, *Divine Direction*. Grand Rapids, Michigan: Zondervan/Harper Collins Publishers. First printing December 2016.

Hansel, Tim. "Pain is inevitable, but misery is optional. We cannot avoid pain, but we can avoid joy" (quote). Goodreads website. Accessed June 15, 2020. www.goodreads.com.

Shakespeare, William, "My Heart is at Your Service" (quote). Goodreads website. Accessed June 15, 2020. www.goodreads.com.

Dr. Seuss. "Sometimes you never know the value of a moment until it becomes a memory." Goodreads website. Accessed June 15, 2020. www. goodreads.com

Unknown. "If you're alone, I'll be your shadow. If you want to cry, I'll be your shoulder. If you want a hug, I'll be your pillow. If you need to be happy, I'll be your smile. But anytime you need a friend, I'll just be me" (quote). Daily Inspirational Quotes. Accessed June 15, 2020. www.dailyinspiration-alquotes.com

Vujicic, Nick. *Life without Limits*. Colorado Springs, Colorado: Waterbrook Press. 2012.

Warren, Kay. *Choose Joy-Because Happiness isn't Enough.* Grand Rapids, Michigan: Revell; A Division of Baker Publishing. 2012.

CPSIA information can be obtained
at www.ICGtesting.com
Printed in the USA
LVHW070803150920
665914LV00008BA/17